I0892107

It Swings from Side to Side

It Swings from Side to Side

James Liddy

ARLEN
HOUSE

It Swings from Side to Side

is published in 2011 by
ARLEN HOUSE
an imprint of Arlen Publications Ltd
42 Grange Abbey Road
Baldoyle
Dublin 13
Ireland
Phone/Fax: 353 86 8207617
Email: arlenhouse@gmail.com

Distributed internationally by
SYRACUSE UNIVERSITY PRESS
621 Skytop Road, Suite 110
Syracuse, NY 13244–5290
Phone: 315–443–5534/Fax: 315–443–5545
Email: supress@syr.edu

ISBN 978–1–85132–023–3, paperback

© Estate of James Liddy, 2011

The moral rights of the author have been asserted

Typesetting ¦ Arlen House
Cover Image ¦ Patrick Inglis Melia

CONTENTS

"I Dreamt I Dwelt in Marble Halls"

My dream in the roots, curlew sound a cafe
– drifting with some I know. Tom Moore's lilt
packed curlew-plaintive marble-cold … Post-dream
trauma comes: no more listening, songs will have
travelled the floor gone through the walls.

Shall I swim the dark route under the waning
lighthouse to the Isle of Man, the island of dogs?
Then I remember Father's Peugeot on another coast,
I braked the car to hunt for bits of songs; curlews
began intoning through Corca Baiscinn's mist.

Under the sea wall down to Philip II's sunken
liberation galleon the sounds kept me marooned
all August nights in Kilkee: loneliness so still
such is the kingdom of souls. The regions' music
escorts of the dead comingled sea and seaweed …

I remember mother's brown bread and oysters
in The Red Bank, I remember Lord Wicklow's
whiskey brown bread oysters in the Bailey,
Kavanagh and Anne Yeats also there. Anne's
question, "Mr. Liddy, would you like another

gin and soda?" I held my glass towards that estate.

LET'S CONCENTRATE, JEFF

I talk on love tired of it
but what's my theory?
Clare was in love with herself
(see her put lipstick on
in her mirror), the fight
against England, the 9th or
19th hole clique, her friend,
her son. Distracted Clare
still thought "James",
she called me "Peachie",
kept this going as she
was stricken. Not holding
down dinner or drinks
she smiled, poor woman
out on the roads no one knows
where one peers at shadows –
what about love then
its fluidity its urge
its end in abandonment!
I pick up theories in the
glitter of Gospel page.
Who was she as she
died in Summer?
The car stuck in Arklow
I forgot she was sick
I phoned home, she got a
mechanic to the parking lot.
Did Clare believe as I do
love is blind and spiritual
and alive the while?
All these are yours O Absalom!
"In love" too the god
Mercury at the crossroads
with eye-flare sticks of fire

though we're set in the womb ...
us with womb eyes on the roads
us shadowy moonlighters ...
I gaze towards you O Absalom!

FRUITFULNESS

I lay there in my mother
as bad a Catholic as her,
they drove back from Dublin
they listened in the car
to foreign radio stations.

A fetus warped enough
to be a medieval fortune hunter
vowed to ineluctable things
blessing itself purging itself,
beseeching attention,
pre-disposed to drink as much as her.

Afterwards the close bosom
of a maturing mother,
warmer days and nights on the radio.
The foreign quality of our adventure from the start.

In Bed in the Morning

He hopes everything will go on as before, the day keeps together, he keeps together. He thinks the churches are open for Mass, he won't go, he should join his intention to the saying priest's. He thinks of his father and mother waking up in bed lighting fags the first thing they do, then they order breakfast. He considers they may be in Purgatory, he will pray for them later. If he is lucky today he will perform accidentally or by inspiration an act of love towards another. Crushes on A-B-C-D-E etc. come to mind; they seem vivifying if not very solid, in some ways they did not become validated. Questions arise: what was left out of these desire/affection encounters and could he have done better, less fire, more sense? Lord, help not my unbelief but my carry on. If You gave me a sexual affinity did even You know what its aura its nimbus referred to? He regrets his eloquence. Write down, he says to himself, what you have been unfaithful to, your betrayals, he will scribble that list later. He makes a resolution, be mindful of a saint once a day or more concretely one who should have been known as a saint. He admires the masked rebels Dedalus, Godot, Gulliver in his own backyard, and over the water mind-climbers such as *In Remembrance of Things Past* and *A Sentimental Education.* Summer: palest of blue skies when he went to piss at dawn, now at noon bursting screaming leaves on trees. There is no excuse for anything but maybe not yet.

He came into the world (John 1:10)

Everyone comes into the world usually in their early twenties, they make their way painfully out of youth. The world looks at them carefully, you have to decide/touch/ marry something. The question is: are you groomed, groomable? Participants come in two ways, those who glide along successfully or hang around; and those who arrive at roundabouts, who weave in manipulations of the real. The former tell stories but you've heard them before; if they chatter about the spiritual it's on family or exercise or magic mushrooms, inner clueless light. The second group, whether silent or voluble, press inside themselves recognition of a journey and monitor a passageway connected to other space. They seek to travel that distance.

Night in Georgie's

Someone sang, "Oft In The Stilly Night". A Limerick said, "I think that's quite beautiful. I'm not much of a patriot, lads, I prefer this to the National Anthem in pubs". Another Limerick, "The National Tantrum, you mean".

I have to recite, I think of Yeats's, "Parnell came down the road, he said to a working man ..." "That's not the original, you know ..." Bridie, Georgie's wife, speaks up, "Ireland will get her freedom and I will still wash glasses".

A new song on Cosheen by Sonny Hastings about a village man, Paddy O'Brien. "He was lost early in the year. He went down to pick up sluacan and was washed away. I was searching for him for nine days. He turned up near the slip".

The doctor during the singing of "Down by the Hillside", "I'm only a student passing through".

Voices piled on, "A song sung by my grandfather 'Snow and Roses'". "I'd like to sing a very old song".

George, "There must be a bit or a piece of an amhráin down there". Martin, "There's great talent down there".

Martin going up to get another pint from Bridie, "God bless you, you have a fine pair of legs".

Outside on the street.

"It was a lovely drop of rain".

"I like a drop myself but only now and then".

"But, Mary, it was very dry".

I get up enamoured of the night's alcohol which I piss out, within the curtained light that has held now for some hours, I remember the party on earth where we write, with gratitude. I recall the "night-school of love" where we find something to write. I am reminded what has blessed me, that I am farther ahead than I was last year at this time in being able to give away alms from my mind bills from my pocket, for struggling with how I am to make a shine and rain of the impulses felt in childhood and since then. Have I said the Confiteor, a clarification of purposes as I put Ireland and its connections to one side? I bequeath my land back to the shanty house of the womb my first room.

Then agile on my feet the day sprints along with its glades scanning the horizon. Angel noon-time with the bell from Peter and Paul's, I drift to allegorise my senses. The angel that floated to Mary and asked the right questions may come to anyone (I leave to one side politics which is marriage or same sex marriage?), here is invitation and sacrifice as we need it. We must shove our hearts to pray in general, we that are only partially the laden and oppressed. I knock the Confiteor on my chest in dismay for the Iraq butchered and seek the route to traveling poor in heart. With this absolute poverty I want to endow my schedule.

I bare myself to Monsieur B who was born into the world of Ennui but taught himself to overcome it with the beauty of caresses, ramshackle caresses. Do I touch a low point but the poet was described as having something of a priest and an artist something ineffable, maybe it's playtime now but I can see Sweetheart and myself as Roman Church priests without benefit of seminary or is this seminary? We've thought of being a priest, I think of religion therefore I am a priest. If we could rake over our hormones our love noise as gifts from Paradise which they couldn't do in the 19th century, not even on the Left Bank, and which we can do only jokingly. Let's throw our Bohemian rags away, God is a rag merchant who walks the smaller streets. Venit Cafe.

AT THOR/HELICON

Come, we have to defend the spirit world that exists beside the bog and bog cotton. To arms against the sports journalists, the folk on TV studio chairs, the 1916 toffs. Come on, let us talking behind their backs nodding with our prompt eloquence vanquish them. Their frugal fantasies threaten us, they hack on to the sportive liturgies of being victims, they put it around priests and poets are short change characters in pulp fiction. We are concealed in the dust they walk over. Even if they forget their rosaries let them keep their noses buried in the tabloids.

Sanctuary lamp from the window, mouth, breast, or hand, keep their tirades out of the pure places, spirit lamp from poet's window, allow us the lustre to pour wounds' blood into our wildflowers as we have done. The lamp Mr. Colum invoked at Thor/Helicon, Mr. Colum for a moment owl-like in the air among the birds' eyes or hovering in the exact nests from which emerge a landing, a clearing, a finishing of hurdles.

The big oak and beech down on knees beg a blessing of the hazel. Tower to sky, squat stone cascade, moving river down into weeds, two three cottages reliced out of attic Bohemia. Poet's boots on stretch of road. The country people couldn't remember that sound or didn't want to – some thought gentry, what are they doing here after the Treaty, some thought amadán, but anyway the poet left. What passed through a few heads was how their grandparents described the dual crowd monumenting Raftery's grave: teachers, county councillors, pub men, riders to hounds, Lady Bountiful of Coole of the windfall apples, gravediggers, all gabbing.

Big dance at Kiltartan's crossroads. Big Smoke plenipotentiaries, cars loaded with pensions, Italian car with beautiful lady professor, cavalcade of publisher and Borges translator, Americans from Molly Glynn's Gort hostelry, Anglicans in shy hiding, the youthful Arts Council and its Jesuit, a literary curate "to the glory of God", rumour with a Roman collar runs wild, "The Bishop's not coming". God sent good weather.

Along the stone wall a flock of bards. Towards them as though towards a line of eternity, from under the thicker trees, bands of colleens with trays of sparkling bumpers. Mead served in the national costumes of green and white (lately fashioned, previously yellow and white Papal blouses and scarves). The bards sat in Tara-like chairs as if on a sun deck. A sup. Mr. Colum in a grey-green pedestal suit, Austin Clarke in black coat broad hat, Tom Kinsella in glasses, John Montague in stammer, on pedestal sixteen me the latest dauphin. In my art and ragged sweater. Beside a summer wall, not as voluble or as bold as the Sliabh Luchra poet-princes, shading our eyes from the strong light with a little draught we hear them and Merriman, lost catches.

Be disappointed, the arch poet is not present, he's lurking in the unsorted Bohemia of Grafton Street. Paddy Kavanagh is unenrolled here the unDolmened one (publishers are dark swans that sing on the Rhine or the Corrib). For security reasons, only posh language in the vicinity of Coole; chair avatars might become aware of a spotlight switch.

Suddenly Mr. Colum steps up straight as a small chapel, in a monotone quavery low and sweet with

Longford brambles and New York sidewalks, he signs into the air a poem stronger than all of him – a maiden's quiet evening, a milking of cows, an accordion accent none may inherit, a tiny water dropping on a stone in the river, the last soft touch of the Nation, ups and recites, "SO THE CROWD COME THEY CARE NOT WHAT MAY COME".

Their music blasts, their prescriptions in the Mall every month renewed, their boundaried gender and identity in the parking lots, soap and soap opera of their children.

I bowed to the tower, to the lamp in the window, to Milton's tower-lamp. I will not forget that line in its hidden choir of collars of gold, I took out my heart and offered it to whatever Anglo-Irish pyramids there are. So did all the bestiary toiling down the road.
Trees intoned into the tower's stairs, dims, and stars.
The water intoned under the bridge. Bequeathed shrine.

Notes for life after that. Desire in the dark kitchen, bar script at close, after midnight endurances, dawn interdicts, cover charges, hot Iberian winds, ocean resort houses, lips and fingers wondering what they're doing, accusations about everything, lingering but knowing definitions. Minerva, order us a round.

Moore Hall and the Fairies

Why am I enraptured by you, George Moore, since if you were clever you were crotchety, if you were a great writer you also did it very badly, soso as novelist as autobiographer the cream? Why am I spun around like a dervish by some of your beautiful sentences since you were not in the front trenches that changed the imagination like Joyce, Yeats, Beckett, you were on the home front in the reserve with very good writers like Bowen, Stephens, Synge, O'Casey, Fallon, and Kavanagh. I could not resist a man whose self-portrait was "... a blasé roué like me, rotten with literature and art ..." I've had a crush on you, taken a shine to you, stuck with you since I was the classical teenager playing classical music in the middle class house. "House" is perhaps the key word though "music" represents the dance you led.

It is the "dream houses" that come upon us when we were young that sets this tone. I had two of them, one on the West Coast another on the East and I still have these dreams, the rooms people used; their voices among furniture and vases. I also seem to be occasionally carried in sleep towards certain shrines (Thor Ballylee dropped out of the list when it lost its cobalt blue to tourist cream); few have appealed more than Moore's Palladian mansion, "the square house on the hill to which the peasants came every morning to work". The pile by the bog by the lake was far larger than my two places put together, it was the palace that stayed in his mind as a symbol of cultural seduction which he did not visit, did not repair but which he kept recalling. Politics hates beauty: with unerring judgment, he left it to Ireland to wreck his house.

In the academic discussion of the theme of "The Big House", Moore Hall stands preeminent. Partly because its owner was enthralled with it and with the idea of subverting that feeling. It was not a great house per se except through the craft Moore brought to the worship and loathing of it. Elizabeth Bowen described it, "While it stood classic and bare and strong the house embodied that perfect idea of living that, in actual living, cannot realize itself. The inside, in proportion and decoration, was of Renaissance simplicity. It was (someone said) a house built for hot days; the ceiling must have reflected the lake light". On the other hand, Moore's life could be seen as the hot house variety in descent from Baudelaire. Incidentally, Elizabeth Bowen might have shared Moore's ambivalent loyalty to her "big house"; she left it to Ireland to axe it by an unofficial route.

But then Moore was not an Anglo-Irish writer, for all his pretensions "Anglo" is not the right word to fix him with: his roots in place and memory went deeper, not to mention his comedic brand of Catholicism. His autobiographical work can be the crossing point between the colonial and post-colonial; this theoretical sequence is lodged inside his own mood swings. Moore's early if interrupted non-residence from Ireland constitutes a foreshadowing of later more famous exiles and of later attitudes among Irish intellectuals, for instance Sean O'Faolain's *The Bell* owes more to Moore than to Yeats and Gregory. His break with the Irish Renaissance opened up the model of an alternative non-nationalist non-provincial ideology, an advantage Patrick Kavanagh discussed. He wrote that Moore was Irish and Catholic and European and possessed a wider range of influences and possibilities than his peers. From this viewpoint it looks as if Moore intended to allow to the Irish Renaissance what he considered he did not need, a tweedy aura of twilight and fields.

For all his unstable character, Moore's dissent on cultural issues allowed him to balance his partisan sense of the Enlightenment with his inheritance from the wild County of Mayo. I contend, however, that he did not allow himself to interact with immediate local traditions in a way that would have permitted greater range as an autobiographical writer: what goes missing in Moore's legacy is intrinsic attachment to folkloric instincts or contexts. His idea of cultural renewal became embodied in an abstract campaign for the advancement of the Irish language but he had no ear or appetite for what the real social imagination of the people, "the peasants", consisted of in pubs and fields. His domineering house and its landscape with its associations and his negative assumptions about it did not bring him closer to what can be variously termed Tara, the Hidden Ireland or the cottage hearth stage. He let Gregory and Yeats manage too ornately (not in terms of poetry but of cultural commentary) the mythic and folkloric deposit at the end of the 19th century. His house was haunted by enough ghosts, presences shall we say from outside the family but dependent on it. He did not much interview his Irish basement. Hy Brasil was lost.

"I came to give Ireland back her language", Moore intoned. Which language? He should have utilized quasi-realistically the dimensions of historical Irish folklore, the concept of an other or a parallel world, the power in spells, fairies, the plaudits of magic. I am reminded of Beerbohm's cartoon of Yeats introducing Moore to the Queen of the fairies: such surprise, bewilderment, coupled with sly guilt and faint nostalgia. The writer confessed, "I listened to the singer but could catch only a vague drift of sound, rising and falling, unmeasured as the wind soughing among the trees or the lament of the waves on the shore, something that might go on all day long ..." Alas! The actuality is Moore Hall stands burnt and bereft, Lough Carra waits in its swans and authorial ashes on an island. The bones of the great racehorses that rested in the stable are in the ground. In the new cottages the descendents of tenants watch TV beside the looted Moore Hall art objects. The fairies are gone, or are they? Moore incorporated in the late fiction story telling techniques that neatly worked in their evocations of Mayo and Galway; he was vibrant as a lyrical writer about these landscapes. These areas are more underpopulated in the fiction than they were in fact. He could have emerged as an stronger realist, outsmarting Gregory at dialect performances and Yeats at the incantation of seers. Perhaps in *The Untilled Field* he came closest. Perhaps he did listen to the chatter of servants and local storytellers and heard more than racing lingo but Moore insisted on being more upstairs than downstairs, though he could be downstairs in other people's houses.

This summer I returned to Moore Hall and found the gates emblazoned with plaques gone, a picnic area in its place. Who has taken the gates – Sinn Fein but they contributed most of the plaques, a Government agency to make Moore Hall prettier, or are the fairies running the show? Nowhere near Moore Hall is George Moore's name mentioned; the descriptions on the gates used to refer to the Moore family's devotion to Ireland from his great uncle John Moore the President of Connaught to his brother Maurice Moore founder of the Irish Volunteers and Free State senator. Maybe the fairies and George Moore together, met or reconciled at last, managed to slip away the semi-relevant inscriptions?

If he was our Henry James his best sentences ring better.

Let the inheritor of Moore Hall have the last word. "Ireland being a fatal disease, fatal to Englishmen, and doubly fatal to Irishmen". Trebly fatal to Americans, I might add.

Anatole France, "The only honest man to emerge during the war was Karl of Austria; but he was a saint and nobody listened to him".

At four he sold fruit and plants from his child's garden to help those on the streets, put his wardrobe out on the street. His great uncle gave him the Order of The Golden Fleece; reading it he remarked the rules were out of date and impossible.

Ate meat only at breakfast, denied himself alcohol for duration of the war only a warm mineral for his heart, no death penalty for deserters or even mutineers, commuting death sentences on Czech radicals by Austrian courts martial, no bombing of cities by his planes.

Against the U boat campaign (if the Americans come in there will be no Kapuzinergruft Capuchins), against Lenin going home in a sealed train (he told the Kaiser that it was unfair to the Russian people).

Joseph Roth, "We could easily demonstrate from Germany's history since Luther that there was an entirely organic, natural, even self-evident progression by way of Frederick II, Bismarck, and Wilhelm to Hitler ..."

So Schonbrunn November 1918. Shivered by the heat from the great porcelain stoves everyone rushed from room to room. Admiral Horthy, shivering, tears, "I will never rest until I have restored your Majesty to your thrones in Vienna and Budapest". Princess

Melaine Metternich, 86, "Tell his Majesty not to worry, revolutions come and go". They go in six cars.

Eckartsau March 1919. Hunting lodge in deep wooded meadow, shooting in the woods for dinner.

Solo dash disguised to Budapest to claim from Horthy The Regent. Karl, "You swore an oath to me", H, "That is no longer valid, it's been superseded". K, "I have released no officer from his oath. And you are also bound to me by a second and more personal oath – that of a court official". H, "Give me a few weeks".

Second dash with Zita in a private plane seated right at the back behind the wings over the Bavarian Alps, stalled at a railway station.

Where will the British dump them, Malta, Ascension Island, Madeira?

Up in Monte it's damp, no electric light smoking green wood in the fireplace, fungus on the chapel wall, a day's walk down, can't afford ox carts or cars, Karl walks down with Otto and Adelheid to buy toys for Karl Ludwig he's four, refuses a coat when someone runs up with one on the way back, chill mist in the trees, pneumonia turpentine camphor and caffeine injections plasters of linseed with mustard bags, oxygen fetched from the hospital.

Too weak to lift the Crucifix the boy Otto brought him.

"Ave Maria gratia plena ... Unser täglich Brot gieb uns heute ... The November manifesto is null and void since I was forced into it, no man can take away from me that I am the crowned King of Hungary ... Let's go home ..."

In Monte cafes in the Square, steps up gardens to the church accordions of Funchal, but a Capuchin brother with a crucifix?

Prayer above Funchal

Out of it comes the sublime. I want the sublime. There exists no other measure or stress.

A South African taxi driver took us up a mess of lush hilly roads to a tabernacle worked in silver over the altar sheltering a small cloaked statue, I am a shepherd I am a shepherdess.

Nossa senhora, speak to me in English (English is an illusion of the sublime). She is speaking in Crown of Stars English, she is speaking through each star.

Did she speak to you in English? Silver English? In Summer, in Monte?

Fleadh 1962

Fleadhs are simple events. The business gets done. I am curious to know what happened on any day.

The ice cream parlour (not factory) brimmed with musiclovers, new pot smokers, McDaid's entire crew. The ice cream disappeared as soon as you entered... A temple of the arts at this moment. Outside a Guinness heir in an Aran sweater asked the crowd, "Are there any good people who can change a hundred pound note for me?" Through the door came Tom Kinsella and Eleanor, the owled second best poet in the country. Leland Bardwell ambled through to the trestles in the backyard. The country's first poet entered groaning. Nods over craters and chasms. Tom inquired what were we having? Paddy was instant, "I wouldn't take a drink from an upstart like you". The rest of us got what we ordered (we knew who had won that round).

The scene drifted to anarchy, orgy... Paddy sitting on the kerb talking to a few children. I invited people to the house and there were musicians playing through my parents' rooms (they were in Kilkee). Soon to be famous performers roamed. Do I remember the name of a young Leo Ransome? Paddy didn't show up as he threatened (in his next column in *The Farmers Journal* he wrote I had turned him away from my door like a dog).

Breakfast time in town, the Main Street was littered with shape-filled sleeping bags. A funeral passed down the street, it was Mrs. Peters, the owner of the Railway Hotel. People woke to say it was the biggest funeral they had ever attended. Paddy came from somewhere, still standing. "Take me out of this fucking kip to Dublin". I wheeled the car round. The poet pissed several times under trees on the road, the last one before The Beehive. On the Bray bypass, Paddy groaned again, "Take me back to Gorey". A limit has been reached. I'm no longer Apollo's chauffer or powder puff, "Paddy, it's time to get out of the car". The poet complied and shuffled off down the street towards The Dargle Tavern.

Driving is long, art is short.

Festivals are from Athens, poets from Sparta.

Dionysius is absolute, Bacchus is morose.

Mo Sweetheart

My love if you have gone back to Grafton
or to places between the freeway and Kit Nash's
you didn't leave until you had put weakness
in my heart's box and if the lake rides in blue waves
I cannot swim an inch more in love's small foam

You deserted me for blonder hair for Goth clothes
for sitting a black-draped statue in The Comet
why did you desert me for one or two women
for playing bass in a band for gliding down
to Chicago's clubs or for the Mad Planet weekend

your bright yellow hair and your glasses that made
you look like T.S. Eliot and your smooth mouth
where Smokey Mountain talk flowed with the pints
I was great with you long baptisms of the week
and we tethering under the sweep of our brains

melted in anecdote dissolved by front seat
goodbye why did you not drive at high speed in
your Swedish car out of the South Side away from
your women "ar do sweetheart" pint-stranded
in the pub Masspath laments across my face

"Mo Sweetheart" far from sharing a pint and
you have left me on the Lake Michigan rocks
of treachery when you stole away in March
to wander about that desert with the kisses
of another friend amid the dew of the cactus

I hope to Mary's kid and to God's only kid
I sleep soundly without your nimbus lit in my mind

– A Tory Folk Song

A bheith i ngrá le fear
(Ó Searcaigh)

Recited by a Fairy Over the Grave of Jonathan Swift

"In Tara's halls
the Divines were bards polling
in dark booths at light
barhopping in the sky ...

an incomparable
incompetent butterfly like me
has words, 'Mr. Dean,
indignation lacerates me

as I drift holding
to a non-doubting regimen
of transcendence,
safe conduct please for

souls in the ancient sense
who travel the Norman rivers
who stir soft altar manners
chalice blood songs

of druids and priests:
the butterfly in the monstrance –
we call it a sunstorm –
in charge of this business'".

Banged on A Bloomsday Accordion by the Fairies of Ballylee Over Lady Gregory's Headstone

Visits of company
Saturday night screeching
into Monday old young
mixed in dance sets

Fling in the knoll
thanks be to Powers
shuffle of whiskey struts
second thirst sight

Human lady with pantry
and wineglasses gives
tenants freedom to pick
apples under the boughs

"Such a handsome
petulant boy
long ago", Gregory
you didn't bankroll

the sheer joy of a young
burdened Dedalus
reading and making out
(we made out we read)

Joy sick & advanced
in nothing & too much
side effects nonchalance
the glare of local trash

A Newsreel

"They never let us write on David Prince of Wales",
the Irish Republican said. "But I'm going to do it".
Churchill in the Commons, "... incoherent and
seemingly the worse for drink, he pleaded on
behalf of the King until he was shouted down".
Rituals of monarchy they toss like salads but the
Republican admires anointing with ice and fire,
the day of oaths, altar soul. Men and women for
summers courted the Prince of Wales in their sleep
half sleep via ascent from Castle to state intimacy,
a spiky dewy path with an American fruit fly on it.
They lay on beaches thinking of him in bright light.
The crown is made of leaves out of life joy-light:
ancestor-pour, libido-pour, the divine quarantines.
The Irishman liked David in his glass cage stance.

All My Days Were Honeymoonish

I learnt America's secret
they don't move in a sphere of light
they're monogamous
they're romantic about something
they know all the time.

Knute in bar light flowing our faces
like smoke in heaven,
"Are you serious about being indifferent
to sex to some extent these past four years?"
"Just stay erotic,
you don't have to bedroom it",
I who Christmas dance twelve days
with Baudelaire a Treeman whose arms
and branches hang with Dante's desires?

American orgasm isn't paradise
my kind of marriage is
sidelined
but I travel to camel breath and luxury
of interrupting an irredeemable,
can I record a Jansenist song?

The time of being a pre-child
during that time of being made ready
for diving and grasping of the ideal friend
who lies same space same feeding
not far away,
starting to fire kiss ...
God wept with happiness on the Tree
because he saw birth was so strong
it could carry the promises over and over.

1997–2008

For a Lover's Honeymoon With Someone Else

A 15 minute/15 day Valentine
you go to San Francisco
to Ocean Beach. In the tram past
the medical school to sand and debris
to where Spicer plugged a transistor ear
to the Giants. The beach bar stools
face a nautical WPA mural,
stamp your postcard with driftwood skin
to my shadow body.

Get soaked. Valentines
are literature. I'm in the County Clare pub
thinking of Bishop Rogers's recitation
of Merriman's *The Midnight Court**
(a colloquy of lascivious bitching)
to the palace's back garden bushes.
The Bishop whiskey-faultless
for nearly a thousand lines:
men come no more the rake minstrel
the Ordinary radiant as scalding.

Can I compare this Valentine
to a Spring or Summer day
and to *Luke* 14. 22,*
"Anyone that comes to me and doesn't
hate father, mother, wife, children, brother,
sister, and not only them but his own life,
can he be my sweetheart?"

* read the book

Ronnie Drew

Your voice was grave but the moral tone of your voice in conversation was Jackeen populist. You rivaled the Pogues with the help of Yeats. You strung out his poems/ballades at the Sligo Festival; Liam Miller gave me the tape which I have somewhere (which country?).

I want to talk about the McCartans the people you married into. Pleasant Deirdre, daughter of Dr. McCartan first envoy to the US. I constantly passed the Newtown Mount Kennedy house with his presidential slogan on the wall. The election was early fifties the whitewash stayed on.

Your brother-in-law Paddy looked after his dying father, I hope he's alright. Did he become a judge? Their New York mother; she told me that my great uncle James Reeves endowed a Fordham University Irish poetry chair for Joseph Campbell.
(Ronnie had attitude too and that carries a voice on crackly golden beams into eternity).

Vacations for Children

Children think of pitchforks. Holidays become assaults on the young. There is car, road, map, two opposing views in the front seat. Never lean forward much to listen.

A place. Irish road uneven and bumpy uncompetitive with hedges that loom high nothing visible except an occasional cow other side of a field gate.

Front seat male titan on tillage. Patches of potatoes and vegetables out the window.

This is across your country.

Specially the country of the female one.

She found Ireland in New York years ago and keeps the details. Porridge tales in the morning, richer evening plates in the evening, the invitation reads, we are a clever talented people; we were victims so spiritually aware.

A Goddess in her own right but with a husband.

Seeing the countryside out of the car window.

A new idea, see the country. An invention of this summer.

The children were used to where they had to go. Summers had been strangely Anglo.

White ocean blanket over rocks. Spray tugged, the Anglo-Irish flora sparkled in return. The stone mouth of George III across the Bay spewed foam at high tide. The villa was built with the boards of a coffin ship the Edmund sinking in sight of the shore (one imagines the pennies of the evicted poor sinking in to the waves).

Children tried to locate a legend, in what room in the 1880s had the whiskered Poet Laureate, the afternoon-tea-mad Tennyson, consumed tea with the Ross Lewin women? Our villa their summer place away from a Shannonside mansion.

The male had his way, the children should see something different. Under her influence they may be turning elegant.

Take them to the country. Show them Achill.

He was the kind of male who thought the family should go driving on Sunday. The female thought they should go a distance, look down a valley, find the public house.

They got into the car and went there.

They had to buy into the Garden of Ireland Program.

"Achill", the map said. Different from what you know. Incandescent near isle reached by a long bridge. She saw a bar at its entrance. She asked for a gin lime and soda. And ice. The publican had never heard of ice. The children learned the standing of ice.

Puzzled children. This was the West, few trees, stone walls, irregular fields. But were not fields larger, trunks leafier? Steeper paths to endless coves and beaches not so many rocks, purple violet haze. Amethystine. Turquoise. Greenish-blue landscape, wild flower patterns.

A word the children thought of "lush". The Lord is my lushful bride.

Diamonds in the waiting water.

Why did the cliffs suggest avatars? A sort of Last Judgment without pain?

Return to Anglos.

The Keel hotel was run by an efficient young Scottish couple. On a mountain above the street stood another hotel owned by Major Freyer. They drove up to it in the car.

Out on the lawn a crowd of young men in costume with bells on their hands and maybe on their toes. Morris dancers, the children's first and last. Their feet skimmed the hillside earth as if it was an English village green.

Summer slow Orpheus Oedipus time by seals and rocks, looking at them from bay windows, in bars by day and night starry perspectives. Now fast time. Clare was a widower and had to be escorted to the West End Hotel or Scotts. She sat with a son and no husband but it was the same tableau since the war. The son was left where he began, womb-sited. The omens sailed into the high tide you could see out the back window of Scotts.

Cousin John a poet on Father's side, was staying with us. He had come up for a few days from Limerick. Dark-haired, tall, handsome, he went around suggesting improvements to the decaying rooms of the house. He looked at the jungle outside, he went to the steep back garden, "You could make a nice vegetable patch here, just a few rows and some flowers near the shed". He considered the line of flagstones outside the breakfast room, "Tidy up the ferns and plants, and put down new ones". Clare had had it. She came down the steps to the street where I was sitting by myself in the car.

"Bring me away from here, the Liddys drive me mad. I can't take another second of this rubbish".

"What places of refreshment do you want to go to?"

"Somewhere anywhere, out into the country". In her golf slacks and pullover she looked desperate beyond belief.

John walked down to the car, "Where are we off to?"

A voyage out the country it was. Where was all this coming from? I bitched into the scene. Silence as I took the wheel on Corca Baiscinn's dusty small roads; we passed the church at Corraclare in its grove of trees and chose one of the pubs on the street. We sat in a corner of its newly timbered lounge. Shaking and twisting I burst at Clare, "I've never got away from you, I've never left my catastrophe the womb, you've kept me locked in, I'm a fucking prisoner, I'm disappearing".

I ran out the door nearly taking it with me, I ran into a field then another one, I pushed through a hedge, stumbled over a bucket. My face fell in the dirt and grass. I crept back slowly and saw the car still outside the pub I stole in and watched Clare and John being friends, I held my head in my heads, I wanted no more from life. I went over to my mother and knelt down at her feet, an exhausted extension of herself.

The cottage was not just children it was the love house the slave house of affection, which they attained after they had spent time scouring hedge and forest for places to merge themselves unseen. The rain had fallen on them so often washing out their touching, they knew very well what a roof was. The possession of the cottage was the ritual of the covenant, they could lie together surrounded in whatever little space by the coming of children's voices. So we – they – lay fairly quietly for the course of centuries. Then the modern: houses and money. The West cottages, small stone walls, wells, and goats, which had pretended to be asleep now contrived to be sit up awake.

Galway was just coming out of the cottage or the back street hovel stage. There were houses, rooms, people were painting them. They had floor space and nooks for intimacies so began the huge era of decoration. The bars too became larger emporiums, lounges added to their front areas But some of the bars tended to resemble cottages, not only because people tended to return to them, inhabit them, but also because love's sorcery was practiced there. The Sawdoctors, frenzied and restrained, brought it back with their melancholy and fun by Lake Michigan. (La Fête Irlandaise stretched up the lake, they could be heard in the distance.) Someone started discussing their refrain about a "Michael D". Several asked who was this "Michael D?" Dave Brannan said, "Didn't you know him, I used to hear you talking about him". "O Jesus, yes".

Galway, wild oats. Kelehan's pub at summer's start: fires getting heaped up with coal in the room facing the hospital, retired R.I.C. men with poitín in upstairs rooms, the cider room at the back for the freaks. Drinks for the police after closing. Mrs. Kelehan would let us stay in the bar if she wanted to go on an errand, we were on the honour system to pay for what we took; the four of us, Michael D, dizzy scattered lecturer in sociology and politician, Brian young Professor of Classics to whom Catullus came in a frenzy after a few, Jim who had come with me from San Francisco a poet temporarily entwined with alcohol and I in residence for a year teaching Lecky and Yeats. We would put the afternoon away like children who wanted to stick around. Jim and I when young were Bohemians but we paid for our drinks. We did, the evening had to grow younger ...

I have to add Jim and I liked a young man whom we called Nora though that was not an accurate personal description. I also add the March moon reigned full. Nora and Jim were discussing the pub and Jim defined it, "This place is like a mental hospital, it's divided into doctors' nurses' and patients' quarters". Nora used to think Jim favoured the patients' quarters at the rear of the pub. We moved freely between the different quarters. Nora had a friend Dorothea who preferred the doctors' quarters that faced the ugly regional hospital across the street. This institution and Kelehan's had an intimate relationship as the pub was the local joy-in-death house, brothel and wake house. The sepia tinted oval framed portraits looked down on the strange group of sinners below.

We were coming to an end of a few hours academic drinking. Michael D entered frazzled carrying a suitcase. He opened it, took out a thick large notebook covered with his writing, "I've just come from the hospital after a short stay and I've written a lot of poems, I'd like to read them to you". I knew he did not mean the hospital across the street. Page by page his whispy voice took over conversation; the hour was here to make our return journey down the Corca Baiscinn coast. Jim had been sitting uneasily in his chair as Michael D intoned; when he paused Dorothea gushed over Jim, Nora was gazing more than a little love sick at Jim. James and Michael D concentrated on Lorca, the far away martyr with green eyes. They fell to the Republican pros and Falangist cons of the Granada event; debate broke out of what led to it; James had read Ian Gibson's *The Death of Lorca* and trumped Michael D, who made a bet James was wrong.

Michael D threatened to read, James began the shuffle out the door, Jim asked Nora, "Will you come to Clare, will you come down to George Fitzpatrick's?" "Yes". Dorothea knew from the moment that she had lost whatever complex game the three were playing. She interjected tragic foreboding her eyes. "Nora, do you have to go?" "Yes". Michael D. "And you're going to leave me in the middle of my reading". We were going down the pavement to the car, the shout hits us, "I'll follow you down to Kilkee and make you listen". We took to the eerie magic coast road in twilight past the castle that fell at the Lisbon earthquake, the bridge rocks and seaweed of Quilty with music blasting out of Casey's pub, to George Fitzpatrick's ultimate two roomed cottage of latest nights, dancers battering on the Liscannor flag floor, and George's cheerful malice floating in whiskey.

We had ordered when Michael D flew in through the door carrying the suitcase with the poems. We shuddered back to the piano and the walls. The customers recognised him from TV. With half hearts we invited him back to the West End house, elegant mid-century Victorian cottage. Party developed, we messed around, Nora and Jim in a corner, Michael D cranky as I produced the Gibson book. Trouble was more than a ghost in the air and I thought I'd leave the complex three together. I heard murmurs then shouts; I peered out the bedroom window and beheld Jim rolling and kicking a sack-like Michael D down the front steps. Standing on the road he lets out roars that could be heard across the Bay at George's Head, "Dirty fucking yank I'll have your head: I'm a member of the Parliament of this country and I have influence. I'll get you deported from this jurisdiction". We went inside as he drove off in the morning light and discovered his case; besides the manuscript a load of drugs for the relief of many kinds of mental pain and suffering.

August 6

In the Mass room at the prayers of the faithful
a short woman spoke, "Today is the anniversary
of Hiroshima, may it never happen again".

Before that the Rector said, "This is the Feast of
The Transfiguration, the anniversary of Paul VI".

At the beginning of the Iraqi War a man stood
in the aisle of the 15 bus, "America, remember
Hiroshima, are you satisfied now?"

During a Gorey Festival stage performance
voices at the door, then Paul Funge strikes up
a pagan dance kicking out his legs between the
seat rows, "Tá sé marbh". ("The Pope is dead").

Feast of the Transfiguration

In The Glen
He is no silver trifle
silver speech bog speech.
They told stories hymn stories in the bog
forbearers cried on their knees
whispered if anyone drew near
the children in bare feet
never ran into the world
(I live in the flesh of my own farm
DNA wrapped in an altar cloth).
The laws were given by others
they could be broken
on clear intent.
Shine or snow
face or garment
these lawbreakers worshipped
and were transfigured
at the Lawbreaker's altar
that stone under the tree,
they came by different paths
changing times so no one noticed,
August 6
stone at the heart of the Glen
God laid on it.
The priest whispered bog Latin
the crowd understood
a stone hovered above in the sky
they knew Christ was no barrack hero
they obtained freedom from the barrack square.

– *Romans* 9:1–5

My Mother's Favourite Poet Was Benedict XV

Osip Mandelstam's Pope with slender figures. Seraph from an almost sawed off branch of a Juniper tree. A bottle of white wine shared with a coachman when the carriage horses bolted in the Vatican gardens.

On the first day ordering anti-Modernist informers' files burnt, on the first day hymns sung for the rejected, the turned-in.

Everyday was All Souls: he extended to priests of the whole world the saying of three Masses on that feast – the first reason for this, the Church owed a debt to the departed in England and Reformation countries where funds were given on condition Masses were said for ever or for a long time. "We are strongly impelled, to supply in some wise, as far as in Us lies, the suffrages omitted".

The second reason, prayer for the dying swan soldiers of the World War, "gone under earth's lid", Ezra Pound, "Charm smiling at the good mouth". Midwestern doughboys, boys of ancient Europe, "We perceive almost before Our eyes such a multitude of men, in the flower of their age, fall to premature death ..."
Ezra Pound died on All Souls Day.

Towards Images of Your Body

A dance with our arms and legs
sweated through your body
saw your chest the garden
with its big flowers and I'm
learning to dance there too
(I would never have danced
except love bade me dance).

The brilliance of such objects
that keep us stretched awake.
This is a zone in which there are
no real questions. Can I have
the next dance and the next one?
Next day you will turn into a
cafe, the bright lights menus.

BURNT NORTON 2

During the week of tests we are on the bed twice
first time tongues in mouths did a wild ballroom,
"Don't think you're going to get this every time".
Next time he prefaced, "I've got one for you, I like
playing the girl". Mouth floor tongues madder.
This is the text for the roses in the rose garden.
Dance ye rosebuds. Dance ye open mouths. I said,
"Sara Palin wears the beautiful legs of Venus",
this is not the text to bring by these garden roses.

FIRST HYMN TO GOD MY GOD IN MY SICKNESS
(through words with Jim Chapson)

"Therefore that he may raise the Lord throws down"

The Bible life, Jesus life, hope life
have been willed

On my plateau these modes are needed
my sweethearts my three books printing

time to loosen the beautiful world
keep the strings

A few knots to be tied elsewhere

Old people may be saints
they're saints gossips in the Cathedral Gesu

Well dressed man at Mass exchanging the sign
of peace exhibited a kind of radiance

Jim tells of his student who was in misery
her father died She saw him in a dream
said he was alright she was happy

Jim's dream in Granville of Paddy McNeice
he wanted Paddy to explain about eternal life
"Don't worry you'll understand it when you get here"

He woke felt better

Commonality people dying in those rooms
be my guides

my father died my mother died

Fun and fire but
glad recent hearts and I didn't walk all the
way on Sperm Road nice to see it

Birth and death the same package
if one is good the other is good
the first was very messy for someone

Fr. Walsh in the Gesu confessional
pours it out "God wants good things for us"
What can a man do for another
hold his hand that assumes a prayer

To follow you
for strength
for healing

sit with Jim Eric Jeff Paul

brides of Christ why not
Brautmystik to lean on Christ's breast

The Song of Songs translated and performed
as being about each of us

Apothegms

Deal with it, the light in which you might be good.

Blue dawn under Tree light, branches of poems.

Birth and death count but love stronger and warmer.

I got to know how to write sentences (I told others), do
not keep sentences isolated.

Kavanagh said the leaves that fall in Kensington
Gardens
are universal leaves, why I have thought of this at the
last moment.

The Tree of poems at the beginning of Creation was in you
so you defended what it is to write a poem, (joined in a
minor way, Pound, Kavanagh, Spicer, Wieners,
Niedecker).

It's right to fall in love if it gives you more
compassion.

The Lord sent angels late, beautiful friends, I will not
name them as they might lose their wings.

15 October 2008

The Interior Rivers of Alaska

Drew Blanchard

For me to write with any sense of objectivity about James Liddy – former teacher, mentor and friend – is impossible. In acknowledging this, I am freed, in some ways, from the initial paralysis that hit me like a train wreck (picture the slow train from Dublin to Wexford. Include a swan or three if you like). My debilitating fears were two-fold: How do I justly present the life and work of a poet like James? And how do I avoid the kind of sentimental trappings that would have raised the ire of James himself? The answer? The book you now hold in your hand. Reading *It Swings from Side to Side* swiftly resolved my dilemmas and loosed the paralytic chains. James Liddy's posthumous collection is a stunning and important book filled with angels, gods and ghosts, with lovers and friends and with family and fighting. Having composed many of these poems after he knew he was ill, James was able to perform a sort of reverse eulogy. To be clear, I am not arguing that these poems are James' attempt to self-eulogize; instead, they extol many of the people that were important to him, both the living and the dead. Through this book he was able to say his goodbyes and to revisit some of the stubborn preoccupations that informed his life and his relationships in this world and beyond. I'll come back to these stubborn preoccupations shortly, but first I must digress.

In a famous letter to Rainer Maria Rilke, the Russian poet Marina Tsvetayava wrote, "You are not the poet I love most ... you are poetry itself". As a poet, Rilke famously lived (in a neo-romantic sense) the life of a poet. Anyone who knew James even slightly knew that he unquestionably lived the life of a poet and artist. James, though, was not just a poet. He was also a cultural critic, historian, and academic (although he was not a typical academic, to be sure). The connection that I want to draw between Liddy and Rilke is not simply their desire to live a poetic life. They are also connected through one of James' "stubborn preoccupations": his mother, Clare.

One of the more infamous biographical anecdotes about Rilke is that his mother, having lost a baby girl the year before his birth, christened him René (a sexually ambiguous name) and dressed him as a little girl until the age of five. I can't help but question how this duality in gender, or more importantly, maybe, his mother's desire for Rilke to be something or someone else must have influenced his unsettled nature in adulthood and the constant longing we see in his *Duino Elegies* and *The Sonnets to Orpheus*. Throughout his life, Rilke had a wandering sense of loneliness: he was never content in one city, never content with one god or the absence of god, never content with one lover or the absence of love. In most of these things, James was very different. James was not an isolationist. And although he did have multiple homes (Milwaukee ... Coolgreany ... Kilkee), he was not a transient and was equally and evenly critical of most places; and James Liddy's mother, of course, did not dress James as a girl or wish him to be something he was not (James' mother did not dress him at all. That was the job of the nanny) as long as he turned out to be just like her. In the opening poem of the collection, "I Dreamt I Dwelt in Marble Halls", James provides a clue to one of the central tensions of the book and of James' life: his relationship with his mother and the lack of a relationship with his father. The title of the poem is borrowed from an aria in the Opera *The Bohemian Girl* by the Irish singer and composer Michael William Balfe. Balfe was born in Dublin, but moved in early childhood to Wexford. James' father later was to become one of the central figures in establishing the Wexford Opera Festival (a social diversion to escape the house and his domineering wife). The title and the melancholy opening of the poem can be understood as a nod to James' father's social escape:

> My dream in the roots, curlew sound a cafe
> – drifting with some I know. Tom Moore's lilt
> packed curlew-plaintive marble-cold ... Post-dream
> trauma comes: no more listening, songs will have
> travelled the floor gone through the walls.

The implied nod to his father in the title and first stanza, however, is trumped by the penultimate stanza and the final, singular line, which is set off on its own, breaking free from the regularity of the proceeding five-line stanzas:

> I remember mother's brown bread and oysters
> in The Red Bank, I remember Lord Wicklow's
> whiskey brown bread oysters in the Bailey,
> Kavanagh and Anne Yeats also there. Anne's
> question, "Mr. Liddy, would you like another
>
> gin and soda?" I held my glass towards that estate.

The estate to which James raises his glass is both a parental choice (mother over father) and a social choice (a life of holding court in pubs and cafés); and like his mother, when James was present, the court was his. This opening poem also gestures to Ireland's creative legacy, a legacy of which James is now a full member. And artistically the use of Balfe's aria extends beyond the allusion to the Wexford musician. References to the same opera appear in two stories by James Joyce as well: "Evelyn" and "Clay". With this tip of the hat to Joyce, James is acknowledging his debt to the Irish writers that preceded him and, simultaneously, adding a new floor to the enormous library of Irish culture (please note my avoidance of a "big house" analogy).

I also can't help but think that the title of Balfe's opera, *The Bohemian Girl*, implies a certain duality that existed in James life. While James certainly followed his mother's love of fine dining and high culture, he was also part bohemian and moved effortlessly from a dirty bar to a four-star bistro. To me, though, what is most astonishing about this poem and much of James' *oeuvre* is his ability to shift the tone of a poem with unnoticed ease. In this particular case, we move from the elegiac, "Tom Moore's lilt/packed curlew-plaintive marble-cold" to the buoyant ending with "brown bread and oysters" and "gin and soda". As a poet James wrote from deep within himself, but he rarely (if ever) leaves you on a somber note. He had the rare ability to balance above his head, Atlas-like, a romantic yearning (without an excess of pathos) and an ironic kick under the table (not too hard, yet not too soft). This balancing act is, in part, what makes James Liddy's voice so unique and contagious: his is a voice that calls you back to hear it again and again.

While the title of the first poem in this collection works so well by layering meaning on top of meaning, the title of this collection is perfect for different reasons. *It Swings from Side to Side* appears nowhere else in the manuscript. I like that. I like it too because it has the salient quality of good titles, the ability to stand on its own and evoke a multitude of images. I will allow you to determine for yourself what "It" is that is swinging. For me it invokes a pendulum and in turn the movement of time: "It" swings back through history and forward to the present and then back again. And the poems in the collection do just that. We move from George Moore's "big house" to the Iraq War and even up to the election of Barack Obama. I should note that James passed away on the morning after the election; and he did learn that his vote was put to good use. I'll end here for fear of that I may move into a mode of sentimental drivel. And I'll end with a quote from James' memoir *The Full Shilling*:

> The passion of Ireland is to talk about people when they are just dead, the passion of North America is to discuss people when they are dead but only on family trees.

I do not claim to know much about too many things, but I know this: when a writer and person like James Liddy passes, people on both shores will continue each night to talk of him until the pub closes.

The rivers of Interior Alaska are described as "braided". The water does not run in one wide channel like those we are used to in the Lower 48, the kind that meander and bend and loop back to themselves in oxbows as they pass through their fertile valleys, changing courses, yes, but so slowly the changes don't register in the marking of time that is our daily lives. In Alaska, the shape of a river is more fluid. Bed and banks are formed of fine glacial silt, a color you can't quite call tan and can't quite call gray. The silt makes the water ashy, opaque; the glaciers make the water cold. The silt is easily pushed, shaped and reshaped, as the water crosses valleys. These rivers flow more like rivulets. Ropes break away and flow back together, forming an unending weave.

ABOUT THE AUTHOR

James Liddy was born in Lr. Pembroke St., Dublin, in 1934. His parents hailed from the cities of Limerick and New York. He lived in Coolgreany, County Wexford, intermittently from 1941 to 2000. His books include *In a Blue Smoke* (Dolmen, 1964), *Blue Mountain* (Dolmen, 1968), *A Munster Song of Love and War* (White Rabbit, 1971), *Baudelaire's Bar Flowers* (Capra/White Rabbit, 1975), *Corca Bascinn* (Dolmen, 1977), *Collected Poems* (Creighton University Press, 1994), *Gold Set Dancing* (Salmon, 2000), *I Only Know that I Love Strength in My Friends and Greatness* (Arlen House, 2003), *On the Raft with Fr. Roseliep* (Arlen House, 2006), *Wexford and Arcady* (Arlen House, 2008), *The Askeaton Sequence* (Arlen House, 2008), *Fest City* (Arlen House, 2010) and *Rome that Heavenly Country* (Arlen House, 2011).

He was a Professor in the English Department at the University of Wisconsin-Milwaukee for many years, where he taught creative writing and Irish and Beat literature. *James Liddy: A Critical Study* by Brian Arkins was published by Arlen House in 2001 and the widely acclaimed *Honeysuckle, Honeyjuice: A Tribute to James Liddy,* edited by Michael S. Begnal, appeared in 2006.

The first volume of his memoir, *The Doctor's House: An Autobiography* was published by Salmon in 2004, with volume two, *The Full Shilling,* appearing in 2009.

He completed this collection, *It Swings from Side to Side,* before he passed away on 5 November 2008 following a short illness. A selected volume is in development.